Leading Self-Help Groups

Leading Self-Help Groups

A Guide for Training Facilitators

Lucretia Mallory

Family Service America   New York

Copyright © 1984 by FAMILY SERVICE AMERICA
44 East 23rd Street, New York, New York 10010

All rights reserved. No part of this book may be reproduced or transmitted in any form, or by any means, electronic or mechanical, including photocopying, recording, or by any information storage and retrieval system, without permission in writing from the Publisher.

Library of Congress Cataloging in Publication Data

Mallory, Lucretia.
  Leading self-help groups.

  Bibliography: p.
  1. Self-help groups. 2. Leadership—and teaching. I. Title.
  HV547.M34 1984   361.7   83-48659
  ISBN 0-87304-206-9

Printed in the United States of America

Contents

PREFACE 7
INTRODUCTION 9

1 ASSUMPTIONS AND DIRECTIONS 13
   An Overview 14
   How to Use This Training Guide 15
   Training Formats 17
      Six-Session Training Outline
      One-Day Training (Seven Hours)

2 SIX-SESSION PROGRAM FORMAT 21
   Session 1 21
      Introductions
      Goals and Establishment of Learning Contract
      Defining *Facilitator*
      Types of Groups
      Leadership
      Positive Leadership Behaviors
      Stages of Groups
   Session 2 29
      Rounds
      Groups as Contractual Entities
      General Housekeeping Considerations

    Basic Needs
    Strokes
  Session 3   42
    Practice Rounds
    Communication Skills
  Session 4   47
    Rounds
    Questions
    Awareness Wheel Review
    Feelings
    Interventions
    Homework
  Session 5   53
    Rounds
    Facilitating Skills Practice
  Session 6   54
    Facilitating Skills Practice
    Problem-Solving Techniques
    Evaluation
    Goodbyes

APPENDIXES
  1. "Training Professionals in Organizing Self-Help Groups," by Frances J. Dory and Frank Riessman   61
  2. Worksheets   67
BIBLIOGRAPHY   *71*

Preface

This guide is the outgrowth of several years' experience in training facilitators for self-help or support groups in Milwaukee, Wisconsin. It reflects the training format used by the author at Family Service of Milwaukee, a social work agency, and the Southside Wellness Project in that city. The format was the basis for a manual prepared with a grant from the Milwaukee Foundation to Family Service of Milwaukee, and this book is developed from the manual.

The training design that is presented is intended to provide an effective learning experience for persons of varying backgrounds who will be facilitating self-help and support groups of many types. It has been used successfully in training groups whose members' levels of education range from a graduate degree to a high school diploma.

Introduction

This manual will be invaluable to facilitators of mutual aid self-help groups. Self-help groups vary enormously in their effectiveness. Facilitators using this manual, together with an awareness of what makes an effective self-help group, can play an important role in developing strong, enduring mutual aid groups.

The following are some of the characteristics of effective self-help groups which facilitators and self-help group leaders may want to consider:

• Groups where there is a strong norm of giving help—playing the helper role—distributed fairly widely throughout the group.

• Groups that have a shared commitment and cohesiveness.

• Groups that don't stand still but rather add new members, allowing the older members to play more of a helper role.

• Groups that have an advocacy orientation, such as self-help for the hard of hearing or single parents. This allows for commitment to institutional change as well as personal help.

- Groups in which there is shared and distributed leadership of various kinds, both formal and informal.
- Groups that provide extra motivation for participating, e.g., recognition, publicity, professional attention, contacts.
- Groups that have an ideology or rationale that explains the problem they are addressing and the methodology for coping with the problem.
- Groups that are dealing with a strongly felt need, problem, or illness.
- Groups that have built definite traditions and structure—meeting at the same time and place, frequently (once a week), providing refreshments.
- Groups that develop a strong experiential knowledge base.
- Groups that maintain some relationship to the professional system from which they may receive assistance, recognition, resources, referral, sponsorship, training, or consultation.
- Groups that have a good balance between the informal, open ethos and the structured dimension related to continuity, group maintenance, and follow-up.
- Groups that provide, in addition to their main agenda of mutual support and help, related activities. For health-oriented groups, this may include various stress-reducing techniques at the meetings or jogging at other times.
- Groups that deal realistically with problems of relapse or regression.
- Groups that believe in themselves, believe that they are effective in dealing with the problems and needs of members.

- Groups that are composed of people with similar background, age level, education, and interests.
- Groups that have access to resources—meeting place, mailing, facilities, phone, publicity.
- Groups that use a variety of behavioral and cognitive principles, either knowingly or unknowingly.
- Groups that are related to a national organization, such as AA, Recovery, Inc., Parents Anonymous, although the relationship may be loose and informal.
- Groups that meet in settings that are reinforcing, such as a senior center or workplace.
- Groups that have at least one and preferably two "energy" people.
- Groups that add a social aspect at the meeting itself and carry out recreational activities, such as parties and trips.

Frank Riessman, Director
National Self-Help Clearinghouse
Graduate School and University Center
City University of New York

1: Assumptions and Directions

Leading Self-Help Groups is not a precisely accurate title for this book. For accuracy's sake, the best title would be *Facilitating Self-Help Groups*. Using *facilitating* in this way, however, would require definition and titles are not the place for definitions.

To *facilitate* means "to make easier." This guide is for the training of persons who have a special role in regard to a self-help group—that of making easy the process of self-help.

To *lead* means "to guide" or "to direct." In a self-help group, leadership is not a function filled by any special person. Leadership moves from member to member according to the direction of the discussion or activity at any particular time in the group's experience.

The process of self-help is based on certain assumptions:

• Each person has the ability to make appropriate use of the available resources to meet needs. Some persons may utilize this ability more fully than others, but it is present in everyone.

• All of us together know more than any one of us.

Everyone has value and has something to add to a group process.
• Each person is the ultimate authority on what he or she needs and on what will work for him or her.
• Open and honest communication is important to a positive group experience.

Accepting these underlying assumptions, we can say that a group facilitator will perform the role best if he or she is a positively focused person with a belief and a trust in the capacity of others to make healthy decisions and act in their own best interests. The facilitator needs skills to communicate these beliefs, and to help create a group atmosphere of trust and acceptance.

Acceptance of an individual should be differentiated from acceptance of all behaviors. A group in which all behaviors are allowed, with no guidelines or limits, may be a group that is unsafe for its members. At best, it will be a group that wastes considerable time. This guide focuses on behaviors and skills that are useful in creating a positive group culture. It presumes that participants in a group will want that kind of culture to prevail and that their behavior will support it.

AN OVERVIEW

This guide will help persons who want training in facilitator skills and those who are doing training of facilitators. The training is designed to provide a basis of knowledge on which potential facilitators can build. It does not aim to teach everything; its intent is to lay a foundation for further development.

Participants will find it a useful point of departure. Their future growth as facilitators will depend on their own initiative in taking advantage of other training, in reading, and in consultation.

The training provides the following:

• A language and structure for thinking and talking about self-help groups;
• Communication skills;
• Practice and feedback as a facilitator in a practice group;
• Affirmation of existing skills;
• Understanding of basic human needs.

The training program in some ways is operated as a support group. However, unlike many self-help and support groups there is a definite agenda and structure. All of us have experience in groups from family groups and social groups to more structured groups. In the training group, the expertise of the participants is drawn on. Members are acknowledged to be authorities on their own learning needs. It is useful for the leader or leaders occasionally to point out to the group how it is similar to and different from a self-help group.

HOW TO USE THIS TRAINING GUIDE

This guide contains the core of material that is made up of lecturettes and explanations of exercises. Leaders are expected to expand on the core materials, adding from their own experiences.

Different groups have different needs. This training may be applicable to your group only in part. You may find it necessary to add to parts of the training to increase its usefulness to your group.

A basic premise of the guide is that no one would undertake the training of self-help group facilitators without extensive experience in working with self-help groups. Within the training sessions, such experience will provide helpful examples and clarifications. A clear distinction between self-help groups and other types of groups is essential. Persons wishing to work with self-help groups should first have attended or observed several groups in an effort to understand the self-help group process.

Trainers of self-help group facilitators need an understanding of the people they are training. They must be able to assess those areas where participants may be biased due to experience with groups other than self-help groups. For example, a background in psychotherapy, either as a client or a therapist, may result in confusion between therapy and self-help. It is essential for facilitators to be aware that analyzing group members' input, probing to "uncover" unconscious data, challenging another's reality, and other behaviors suggestive of a therapist-client relationship are inappropriate in a self-help group.

In a self-help group the process is also the task. Persons whose previous group experience has been with task-oriented groups, where the collective energy is focused on an end product, may be discouraged by the absence of a well-defined end in a self-help group. It is useful for the trainer to emphasize that the nature of help in a self-help group may be a subjective internal shift in perceptions, a sense of connectedness with others in the group, or similar intangibles. Help may be experienced differently by each member of the group. A self-help group may be a successful group and not have one tangible outcome attained by all members.

Although the training in this guide is designed to be applicable to the range of backgrounds one finds in self-help group facilitators, supplemental materials may be desirable for trainees.

Such materials include this guide's foreword by Frank Riessman and the article in the appendix, "Training Professionals in Organizing Self-Help Groups" by Riessman and Frances J. Dory. Our bibliography lists other resources.

TRAINING FORMATS

The training can be done in either of two formats—in a series of six two-hour sessions or in a seven-hour all-day session. The longer format is designed to cover a period of six weeks. The outline for it is presented below. Detailed instructions for the activities of each session are presented in part 2.

- *Six-Session Training Outline*

SESSION 1

A. Introduction
B. Goals and Establishment of Learning Contract
C. Defining Facilitator: Discussion
D. Types of Groups: Lecturette
E. Leadership: Lecturette
F. Positive Leadership Behaviors: Exercise
G. Stages of Groups: Lecturette

SESSION 2

- A. Rounds: Activity and Explanation
- B. Groups as Contractual Entities: Lecturette
- C. General Housekeeping Considerations: Lecturette
- D. Basic Needs: Lecturette and Exercise
- E. Strokes: Lecturette and Exercise

SESSION 3

- A. Practice Rounds
- B. Communication Skills: Lecturette and Exercise

SESSION 4

- A. Rounds
- B. Questions
- C. Awareness Wheel Review
- D. Feelings: Lecturette
- E. Interventions: Lecturette and Exercise
- F. Homework

SESSION 5

- A. Rounds
- B. Facilitating Skills: Practice

SESSION 6

- A. Practice Continues (if needed)
- B. Problem-Solving Techniques: Lecturette and Exercise
- C. Evaluation: Discussion
- D. Goodbyes: Lecturette and Exercise

• *One-Day Training (Seven Hours)*

The one-day training plan is a highly compressed version of the six-week program. Depending on the expressed needs of the group, activities may be added or deleted. The outline presented below calls for activities explained in part 2, which provides details for the six-session course. Exercise 10 is a variation of the exercise in E, Session 4 of the six-session training.

1. Introductions
2. Contracts (Make contracts with members, then explain concept of contracts in groups.)
3. Define *Facilitator*
4. Types of Groups
5. Leadership
6. Exercise: "Positive Leadership Behaviors"
7. Rounds
8. General Housekeeping and Group Rules
9. Communication Skills
10. Problem-Solving Exercise. (Make a list of problems that commonly arise in groups. Break into small groups of three or four people. Each small group will work out several options for handling the problem and then role play within their group. Process solutions as a large group. As time allows, reform small groups and work through new situations as before.)

2: Six-Session Program Format

SESSION 1

- *A. Introductions*

1. The leader introduces her or himself and welcomes participants. He or she tells of personal experiences in training facilitators and working with self-help groups.

2. Introductory Exercises: The leader instructs participants to divide into pairs. The partners are to interview each other to find answers to the following questions: What is your name? Why are you here? What is there about you that you would like the others to know? Allow five or six minutes for interviewing and call time when one minute is left to allow participants to "wrap up." Ask participant pairs to introduce each other to group. Allow about eight minutes for each participant.

- *B. Goals and Establishment of Learning Contract*

1. The leader explains the goals of the workshop from his or her perspective, using part 1, "Assumptions and Directions," as a guide.

2. The leader asks the participants, "Is this what you came for? Do you have expectations that have not been mentioned?"

3. Having learned the participants' expectations, the leader negotiates an agreement between the expectations and the planned agenda. Flexibility will help the negotiation process.

• *C. Defining Facilitator: Discussion*

This discussion is especially important since people have differing views of the facilitator's role. A facilitator is one who "makes easy." What a facilitator makes easy is the process of self-help within the group. This process depends in part on how the group defines self-help. During the process of defining "facilitator," it is useful for participants to examine their beliefs about the potential members of the self-help groups they expect to work with: How will those groups help their members? The leader can ask:

Why will people come to your group?
What will they get from the group that will be useful to them?
How will it be useful to them?
What will you do and/or say that will facilitate this process of help?
What do you expect they will do or say?

The leader should listen for definitions of *facilitator* that are overly grandiose, overly ambitious, or unrealistic. Some group facilitators have burned out because they defined their roles too broadly or set no limits for their own protection. The worksheets on burnout and facilitator awareness that are Appendix 2 may be used here.

• *D. Types of Groups: Lecturette*

(In this guide, *lecturette* refers to an oral presentation by the leader. The quoted material that follows represents such a lecturette. The content is important to the session, but the leader's presentation will be most effective if the material is presented in his or her own words.)

"A group is a collection of three or more people in the same space with a common purpose. In a self-help group, the common purpose relates to ways in which the members can help themselves and each other through a common life experience. Self-help groups may be categorized in a multitude of ways. For example, it is useful to look at self-help groups according to purpose and leadership style.

"The manner in which *help* is defined by its members is one way a group may be categorized. Such purposes may be:

Support
Social Action
Growth/Self-Improvement
Educational
Social/Recreational

"A *Support* group usually defines *support* as a verbal process. It may include sharing of experiences, verbal affirmations of individual members, and acceptance of feelings.

"A *Social Action* group is one in which the energies of the group are focused on making changes in the external environment of group members, by influencing and informing the public or elected officials.

"*Growth/Self-Improvement* groups are focused on change within the individual as a result of experiences provided in the group. These groups may be supportive in many ways; however, they differ from support groups in their focus on change. These groups often have a series of group exercises designed to facilitate the expected change.

"*Educational* groups assume that their members will best be helped by information. These groups often have speakers and a lecture-discussion format.

"*Social/Recreational* groups are organized to provide opportunities for members to get together to enjoy a common activity. The help they offer their members is the opportunity to meet people and have fun.

"Few groups are purely one type; most are mixtures of two or more of these types. However, many groups can identify one of these types as their major thrust.

"Self-help groups, although therapeutic, are not therapy groups. It is critical that facilitators of self-help groups have a clear understanding of the difference between the two. In a self-help group every member is an expert; it is the sharing of expertise gained from life experience that provides members with new options and support.

"The distinction can be reflected in the cost of participation in a group. While minimal dues may be paid to maintain a self-help group, these dues are often optional and are paid to the group, not to the facilitator. In a therapy group the therapist is hired for his or her expertise and is not a member in the full sense of the word. Each member has a legitimate expectation that the therapist will use expertise to the client's advantage in the group. The therapist, by virtue of the contract and the money exchange and his or her knowledge, is the final authority. The therapist will use some techniques in the exercise of his or her profession that would be inappropriate in a self-help group. In a self-help group, the helper role shifts from member to member, thus ensuring that input by all is maximized. It is not appropriate for the therapist to expect to get his or her needs met in the therapy group.

"*Discussion Questions:* Pick some self-help groups that you are familiar with and tell us about them:

"What is their major focus?
"How might help be defined in each of those groups?
"Are the group's activities congruent with its stated purpose?
"What type of leadership does the group have? How does the leadership style in the group seem to relate to the type of group?"

• *E. Leadership: Lecturette*

"It is useful to consider that leadership in self-help groups is a series of functions rather than a person. There are three major leadership functions: emotional, task, and practical maintenance.

"The *emotional leadership* functions are those behaviors that recognize individual emotional needs as they emerge in the group and that assist individuals in meeting those needs. Such behaviors may include giving attention to a silent member, making an empathetic remark to a member's expression of feeling, clarifying and summarizing a member's statements and praising a member's actions.

"*Task leadership* functions include such activities as keeping the group aware of its schedule, making certain that necessary decisions are made and clearly agreed upon, and refocusing the group's attention when the group goes off on a tangent. These activities are designed to ensure that the group as a whole accomplishes what it has stated as its purpose within the limits of time and energy it has defined.

"The *practical maintenance* area is often not recognized as a leadership function. This function includes activities such as arriving early to ensure that the room is open and ready for use, making coffee, arranging for clean-up, and ensuring members are aware of schedules and other information relating to the group and its purpose.

"In the early stages of a new group, the facilitator may find the group members look to him or her to fill many of these functions. As the group matures, members can be expected to meet many more of these tasks themselves. It is useful for the facilitator to discuss with the group very early who will do what and for how long. Many of us are accustomed to being in groups where leadership functions and the role of leader are one and the same. If the facilitator is clear with group members that this is not so in this group, members will feel free to assume needed leadership functions. If the facilitator asks people to identify the behaviors that will make their group successful, the members can gain awareness of these behaviors and will be more likely to use them. The sharing of leadership by all members is one of the distinguishing features of a self-help group.

"The movement of leadership in a group can be viewed on the following continuum:

Leader Dependent	Interdependent	Independent
One or more designated leaders	All members assume leadership as needed	Members no longer need group

"Learning the process whereby people give and get assistance can be one of the most valuable gifts people receive from a self-help group. A facilitator who is comfortable with the group's movement to an "interdependent" phase will make this learning possible."

• *F. Positive Leadership Behaviors: Exercise*

"This activity requires groups of three or four members; each small group is to appoint a recorder.

"Think of a person you know who is a good facilitator. If you have no group experience, think of a friend who is helpful or of a learning experience in which the instructor was helpful.

"Each small group is asked to list all the behaviors members can think of that these helping people engaged in (What did they do? Say? How did they look?). After each small group has made an individual list, write the items on a chalk board using a 'round robin' method. Do this until there are no new items. Then discuss the items in terms of leadership behavior. Check with the group to see if additional necessary leadership behaviors are missing. If so, add them. Ask each of the participants to think of the self-help group that he or she expects to work with and its focus and purpose. Referring to the list on the chalk board, ask:

"Which of these behaviors are essential to your group?

"Which of these behaviors do you expect of members?

"How will you communicate these expectations to members?"

• *G. Stages of Groups: Lecturette*

"Groups grow and change as time passes. If you review the continuum of leadership just presented, you will see one way in which they change. Another way they change is in terms of individual's sense of identification with the group. A dimension that may measure this is called cohesiveness. Cohesiveness is the quality of togetherness that develops in a group. In a positively focused group, cohesiveness relates to feelings of trust and comfort among members. On a time continuum this dimension would look like this:

New Group		Old Group
Low cohesiveness, fragmentation, much "testing the water"	Increased cohesiveness, closeness, trust	Decreased cohesiveness, trust may still be there

"People come into a group for the first time with some of the following questions: What is this group? Who are these people? How will I be treated here? Can I trust them? Will this group help?

"If they are able to find answers and the answers meet their needs and expectations, the group will be valuable to them. If they do not find the answers they want, they are likely to leave. As these questions are answered positively, the group boundaries become tightened, the group's cohesiveness grows. In the final stage, illustrated on the continuum, people have met the needs they came for. They may still feel positively about the group, but it is no longer meeting a need. At this point the group is likely to lose members. Losing members is not always a sign a group has failed. It can be a sign it has succeeded exceptionally well.

"These changes affect the facilitator. Initially, when your group is new, the members may spend time talking about what you will do, how you will do it and why, what your expectations are. The potential for conflict is relatively slight. As members begin to trust each other and use each other's input, you, as the facilitator, may be challenged. Conflict may arise as the group moves from low to high cohesiveness. As the facilitator, you need to remember that conflict is an opportunity for the group to gain greater trust if the conflict is dealt with openly and positively."

SESSION 2

• *A. Rounds: Activity and Explanation*

Start with a round (round robin), using a specific theme or simply asking the participants how their weeks went. Use the activity to introduce a discussion of rounds as a group technique. The discussion should include the following points:

A round is simply the technique of having each group member participate with verbal information about her-or himself in relationship to a topic, a happening, or a question. Usually, members may pass. However, it is important that the members passing indicate that they wish to pass and that they are asked if they want to contribute later in the group. A person who always passes and gives little reason for doing so may threaten group cohesiveness. The reason is the tendency of many people to interpret silence as disapproval. If the persons verbally indicate they do not wish to respond and also indicate whether they will contribute later, the group members have some information and the persons have in fact participated.

- Rounds are a useful opening for groups. They establish the group boundary early in a session. They make a good tool for bringing people into the "here and now" and serve well as ice breakers. Here are some questions that may be used in rounds to encourage sharing and thus to build cohesiveness: "What is one thing you've done in your life that you thought you'd never be able to do? If you were an animal, what would you be? What's your birth order in your family?"
- The most important job of the facilitator in rounds is to keep the action moving. Occasionally, someone will introduce a topic in rounds that captures the interest of the group and stimulates a discussion. Should that happen or should the rounds get focused on one member for other reasons, the facilitator should intervene. An example of such an intervention is "I think what you are saying is impor-

tant; may we come back to it after we have completed rounds?"

- Rounds are helpful when group interest is flagging—when, for instance, there is drop in group energy. The facilitator may wish to express his or her discomfort, thoughts or feelings and ask others to share theirs. It is a good way to find out what's going on in the group. In addition, since a self-help group is one in which all members have some leadership responsibility, involving members in this way is preferable to the unilateral decision making and problem solving that are characteristic of other types of groups.

- Some groups also use rounds to set agenda: "What do you want tonight? What do you want to get done in the group tonight?" Use of rounds in this way gives everyone a chance to negotiate their needs within the group. The facilitator may then summarize the needs expressed, point out the time available, and ask members to set an agenda for the meeting.

• *B. Groups as Contractual Entities: Lecturette*

"Groups are contractual. People come into groups with wants and needs and with expectations of how these will be met. In exchange for having wants and needs met, each member agrees to be available to other members of the group. In other words, members of a group give up some of their autonomy for the benefit of having their needs met. Since groups are contractual, communication about expectations of self, others, and the group need to be clear. Thus far, we have talked about two ways of doing this: (1) the facilitator negotiating his or her role with the group; and (2) clarifying what type of group it is, its purpose, and how the purpose will be met.

"Because groups are contractual, group rules should be explicit and verbally assented to by all members. Verbal assent is important because people tend to take their assent more seriously if they hear themselves expressing it and are heard by others.

"Four aspects of group experience need clear contracting. The contract, with its clearly stipulated behavioral expectation, may then become a rule. These aspects are: confidentiality, leaving a group, reactivity, and expressing wants and needs."

CONFIDENTIALITY

"One rule that is useful in groups is confidentiality. 'What is said here stays here.' In contracting for a rule of confidentiality, it is useful to give precise examples. Some people assume that confidentiality excludes spouses and close friends. It does not; family and friends are not to be told group confidences. Another common violation occurs when group members talk about other group members in public places within hearing of non group members. Well-intentioned members, attempting to keep confidentiality by not mentioning names, may reveal identities by giving other information. These examples should be kept in mind when contracting for keeping the group confidential. Here is an example of a contract for confidentiality. 'Do you agree that what is said or done in the group will not be shared outside the group to anyone, including spouses, lovers, and close friends? The exception is that you may share what you have learned about yourself as long as other members are not mentioned.'"

LEAVING A GROUP

"When a member leaves a group that has cohered, the person's absence can create the sense of a temporary hole in the group; the person's unique input will be missing. In addition, if the person leaves without saying goodbye and giving an explanation, the departure may create an energy drain within the group. The reason is that other members have not had the opportunity to gain closure by saying goodbye, expressing appreciation, and finishing up any issues with that person. In addition, it is not uncommon for members to have negative fantasies about a person's reasons for leaving. A measure to prevent this problem is to ask members to agree on a procedure for leaving. Asking persons to return one time to say goodbye is usually effective. Most people will keep that contract. When someone does not, it may be useful to share fantasies about the absent member's leaving and to acknowledge that they are *fantasies*. Also useful is to introduce some positive fantasies about their leaving, for example: 'Georgia may have gotten what she needed at this time. If she needs more, she knows where we are.' Self-help members should feel free to come and go based on their own needs at the time. The flexibility to do so can be built in easily."

REACTIVITY

"Basically, reactivity means sharing thoughts, feelings, and reactions to the issues and persons in the group. In social situations we are not apt to be fully reactive and to be so may be inappropriate. However, in a self-help group, reactivity is essential. Reactions can be positive, questioning, or critical in nature. Good communication skills and an attitude of caring are essential ingredients in a reactive group. (In a later training session there can be role play and discussion of ways to be reactive with certain common group problems.) Failure to deal with issues in a group also drains its energy. People see the group as ineffectual and may form subgroups in which the group problems are discussed but without a decision or commitment to resolve the problems.

"By contracting with each other to be reactive, group members agree both to sharing their own observations and to listening to and considering others'. It is unlikely that contracting for reactivity will result in members communicating in ways that show trust, caring, and a willingness to be vulnerable. However, the facilitator can refer back to this contract as the group moves in the direction of openness. The facilitator may find her- or himself demonstrating reactivity initially and acting as a role model. As members see reactivity's effectiveness, they will be more likely to engage reactively within the group."

EXPRESSING WANTS AND NEEDS

"Asking for wants is another potential area for contracting with group members. Simply put, this means that each member agrees that if the group is not meeting a need that he or she feels the member will let the others know in the group session and will make a statement about what members can do to meet the need. In this way each individual is acknowledged to be responsible for identifying his or her own needs and verbally asking for that need to be met. Many of us were raised with the notion that others know what we need. Thus, when we do not receive what we want or need, we may believe that others are withholding or do not care for us. In reality, few if any of us are accurate mind readers. In a self-help group where members are acknowledged to be the ultimate authorities on what they need, members also have the responsibility to communicate needs. To decide that the group cannot help without asking for help is unfair to all.

"Identifying needs is unfamiliar for many people. Initially, group members may find the task uncomfortable and may describe a feeling or reaction without clearly identifying a need. If this happens, it is useful for the facilitator to intervene and ask that the person think of ways the group can help. When group members offer suggestions in response to a statement of discomfort without clarifying the need, a process sometimes described as 'Why don't you—Yes, but . . .' may evolve. Such a process often concludes with all participants experiencing frustration."

- ## C. General Housekeeping Considerations: Lecturette

"Many practical issues are involved in planning a group: Among them, time, physical location, introduction of new members, size of groups, and screening.

"Setting the time for the group to meet requires that you examine the life-style of members. If you want working people as members, schedule the group at times when potential members are unlikely to be working. If you schedule early evening meetings, consider the impact on members responsible for feeding children. A very successful group for single parents begins its meetings at 5:15 P.M. From 4:30 to 5:15 P.M. members arrive with their children, many coming directly from work and school. From 4:30 to 5:15 P.M. a light meal is provided to parents and children, and from 5:15 to 6:30 P.M. baby-sitting is provided for the children. Thus, members can arrive home with time and energy to accomplish tasks awaiting them. In contrast, the author once observed a group whose members were divorced women with children that met on a week night at 7:30, did not provide baby-sitting, and often ran as much as an hour and a half over time. This group did not keep members!

"An ideal physical location is not always possible, since many groups try to avoid the cost of meeting space and use donated space instead; one important consideration is accessibility. Is the place accessible to handicapped persons? Accessibility also refers to the ease with which individuals can reach the meeting place. Is it on a bus route? Is there parking? Can a new member find the location without wasting time and gas driving through back streets?

"In the meeting room, lighting, ventilation, and comfort in seating are important factors. A two-hour meeting in a room with glaring light, poor ventilation, and folding chairs will be a meeting in which much energy is lost due to physical discomfort. An ideal room is one that accommodates the members easily, provides good lighting and ventilation, and is equipped with comfortable chairs. The chairs should be arranged in a circle so that members can have visual access to each other without engaging in awkward postures.

"The optimal size of a group depends on its purpose and the type of exchange members are to have. In large groups, more than twelve members, much of the work and life of the group will take place in small sub-groups. In a group whose purpose depends on members sharing reactions, expectations, needs, or wants, and giving support, the optimal group size is between five and twelve members. A group of fewer than five members may have difficulty keeping energy levels high. More than twelve members may mean that some members become 'lost.' In a group with an enrollment of more than twelve persons but with a purpose for which the advantages of a small group are desired, the members might be organized into permanent small groups. The advantage of the permament small group is that it is more likely to result in members identifying with the group and developing trust. If membership in small groups changes significantly with each session, the group process is impeded.

"Assimilating new members in a group is a matter that requires planning. New members in an old group in essence creates a new group. The group then needs to go through steps of establishing trust and closeness and defining roles. To retain a more stable group culture, it is useful to use guidelines regarding introduction of new members. Introducing no more than one or two members at a time lessens disruption. Pacing the introductions at four-week intervals is also useful; it allows the group to reform before further introductions. Inquiring to determine whether group members want a new member affirms the integrity of the group and may work to provide the new member with greater acceptance.

"It is useful for groups to have a policy for introducing and integrating new members. The new member needs to know what the group is about and how he or she will fit in. Likewise, the group will want to know who the member is, why she or he is interested, and how she or he will fit in. Explaining group rules, having experienced members describe what the group has been for them, and having the new member explain how and why she or he is there provide a useful introductory format.

"Some groups feel that they are of greatest value when they admit new members at any time. Such groups have an unpredictable attendance as membership varies greatly from week to week. Often a core group of old members form. They can provide group stability and ensure continuity. However, new members may perceive the core group as a closed clique. If the core group sees its function as assisting new members to understand the entire group and to feel comfortable in it, negative perception is less likely to occur.

"The issue of screening arises occasionally. Many groups have an open door policy; screening is not an issue for them. In such groups, members screen themselves; those remaining will be persons who are in some ways getting needs met within the group. Where sceening is done, potential members may be offered an individual interview in which they are given information about the group, its purposes and rules, how it works, and other essential details. The potential member is asked about his or her reasons for wanting to be part of the group. The interview may be conducted by the group facilitator or another designated person. During the interview, the potential member and the interviewer make a decision regarding the appropriateness of the member for the group. This process allows misconceptions to be cleared up outside the group meeting. For example, a potential member may be looking for a social group and feel uncomfortable at the idea of a support group. Each group will have their own criteria for membership. However, an essential quality for a member is the ability to share. Persons whose need is so great that they take all the group's energy would be better in individual therapy."

- *Basic Needs: Lecturette and Exercise*

"Facilitators cannot afford to overlook basic human needs in working with self-help groups. A self-help group member lacking elements of well-being will not be able to apply full energy to thinking and problem solving. A lengthy group discussion about options for solving a particular problem will often be unproductive for a member who is in a state of deprivation due to lack of sleep or poor nutrition. Indeed, a group facilitator who is not attending to basic needs will have limited energy to put into the group.

"A check list by George Knippel is useful in assessing basic human needs:

Food:	Adequate nutrition, even though in times of stress you may not feel hungry.
Rest & Exercise:	A mix of both. Knippel does not include exercise, but the author of this guide believes it is important to include the two.

Water:	Coffee, tea, and soft drinks don't count.
Air and Space:	Chain smoking will decrease your oxygen supply. Taking time for yourself may be a necessary way of gaining space.
Strokes:	Verbal and nonverbal recognition. Be with people you care for and who care for you.
Elimination:	Not a parlor topic in our culture but necessary.

"Each of these needs can be met at different levels. The optimal level is to anticipate the need and plan for it so as to avoid discomfort. However, some people wait for the feeling of discomfort and then attend to the need. Other people, particularly those in crisis, will refuse to ackowledge the need at all. When this happens, more and more energy goes into the discounting process, refusing to acknowledge the need, and less and less is available for thinking. People at this stage may ramble in talking, seem unable to focus, evidence high level of feelings, or withdraw, appearing listless and drained. Should a group member show these symptoms in a group, the facilitator or other members may find it useful to find out whether the member's basic needs are being met. Attending to them may be a matter of first priority.

"As a group facilitator, assess your awareness of these needs in yourself periodically. Are you meeting them adequately?"

Exercise: Divide into small groups of four to six persons. Have individuals in each group reflect separately on how they are meeting their needs.

The groups discuss how needs can be met and how they can be anticipated. What needs are difficult to plan for and meet?

• *D. Strokes: Lecturette and Exercise*

"The issue of 'strokes' (units of recognition) deserves particular attention. At a time of crisis, sources of strokes may become scarce because people close to us are often also involved in the crisis. Members of groups where loss or separation are issues report that they intensely feel the loss of physical strokes. If you are comfortable with physical touching and members of your self-help group are also, the group may become a place where members can get a hug or a back rub. If not, other strokes can be an important part of the process of self-help—a smile for a member, a compliment, an affirmation of her or his skills in problem solving. All of these are important. Encouraging members to receive and 'take in' strokes is important. Asking members to give themselves strokes or affirmations has been tried in many groups with success. We can try an exercise which deals with getting strokes from others and giving them to ourselves."

Exercise: On a sheet of paper write three of your positive traits that will help you to be a good group facilitator. Now pick a partner in the group. Taking turns with your partner, read your list. Ask your partner to repeat each stroke to you. For example, if you have "I am a caring person" on your list, your partner would repeat it by saying, "You are a caring person." As you hear that stroke repeated, acknowledge it with "Thank you." Really listen and take it in. When you have completed your list, stop and ask your partner to add two additional positive characteristics that he or she has observed in you. Repeat the steps. Discuss these questions: What did you observe about your own process in giving and receiving strokes? Was it easy or hard for you? What did you do or think that made this easy or hard?

Homework: Next week (Week 3), part of the group session will include practice in facilitating rounds in a group. Two members will be asked to participate as co-facilitators in a simulated group. Other participants will be asked to respond as group members and give the practicing facilitators feedback on their use of skills. In preparation, select two volunteers, ask them to pick a topic they would like to use for rounds, and come prepared to initiate the round and facilitate the sharing. (Depending on the size of your group, you may wish to have two sets of rounds, allowing for two co-facilitator teams. This can also decrease the number of co-facilitator teams who would practice in Session 5. If you plan to have two co-facilitator teams, assign the order in which they are to practice facilitating the rounds next time.)

SESSION 3

• *A. Practice Rounds*

"Before the facilitators begin, ask the other members to function as they normally would in the group. After each round, ask the practicing facilitators to comment on what was easy or hard. Ask if they would like feedback. It is most useful to structure the feedback in positive terms: first, what facilitator skills did you think were useful; second, is there anything you would have done differently? Clarify what and how.

- ### B. Communication Skills: Lecturette and Exercise

"The Awareness Wheel represents five dimensions of awareness.* (See Figure 1.) They are data from the senses, interpretations, feelings, wants, and actions:

FIGURE 1: THE AWARENESS WHEEL†

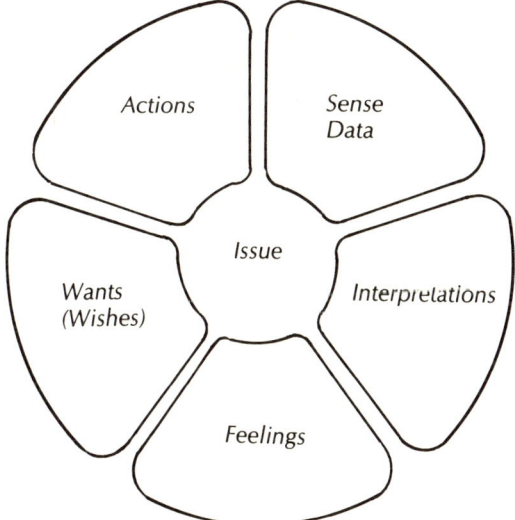

*The Awareness Wheel is a communication tool from the Minnesota Couple Communication Program of Interpersonal Communication Programs, Inc., 300 Clifton Avenue, Minneapolis, MN 55403. *Talking Together* is the participant's handbook for this course. Used by permission.

†Reprinted from *Talking Together* with the permission of the authors and publisher, Interpersonal Communication Programs, Inc., 1925 Nicollet Avenue, Minneapolis, MN 55403.

"Data from the senses include what you can see, hear, taste, smell, and physically feel.

"Interpretations are the sense you make of your sensory data, what you think about what your senses tell you.

"Feelings are your emotions, based on the sensory data and your thinking.

"What you want includes wants for self, for others, and, as facilitator, for the group as a whole. Wants may be conflicting and involve choices and decision making.

"The final dimension is actions. Your actions are the end result of the whole internal process described in the Awareness Wheel.

"To persons other than yourself, only your actions and the sensory data can be known unless you choose to share your internal awareness. The more you share, the more understandable you will be to others.

"The Awareness Wheel is related to issues. Issues for the facilitator of a self-help group will be events in the group's life that need to be dealt with. Examples include a drop in group energy; a rambling unfocused group member; an important, but difficult message you have for a member regarding a behavior that may be blocking the group. Dealing with such issues, facilitators need to clarify and organize their internal awareness. Questions to ask one's self would be: What data from my senses am I responding to? What do I think about this data? What am I feeling? What do I want? What will I do?

"In those instances where a facilitator wants to clarify a member's communications, she or he would ask these questions of a member: What is your data (experience)? What do you think about it? What are you feeling? What do you want or wish for? What will you do?

"To illustrate how a facilitator can use the Awareness Wheel, let's consider a few examples:

"*Group energy has dropped:* Use the parts of the Awareness Wheel to organize your internal awareness. What sensory data do you have about the drop in energy? Do you see people staring off into space? Do you hear short responses or perhaps only the fluorescent light as no one is speaking? What are your interpretations? Do you think members are bored or uncomfortable? or perhaps withdrawing because they are experiencing extreme emotions? Perhaps you think the group is in trouble, and you don't know why. What feelings do you have? Are you scared, concerned about losing group interest? Angry that people aren't sharing? What wants do you yourself have? You may want someone to say something, the group to be energized, feedback on your facilitator skills, the problem to come to the surface. For the group? What will you do? Perhaps you decide to go with the low energy a little longer and see what happens. Or you may decide to share your awareness and ask the group members for their input on the drop in energy.

"*A member is talking about a difficult issue.* As facilitator, you want to focus because the person sounds confused. Check out which parts of his or her awareness you are hearing. Ask about those parts you don't hear: For example, what do you think about that? What do you feel? What do you want?

"*You have a difficult message to send.* You are

anxious to be heard and understood. Use the Awareness Wheel to organize your communication. In confrontive communications, starting at the point of sensory data and being sure to include a want increase the likelihood of success. For example: 'Joe, when Sue began to cry you handed her Kleenex and told her crying doesn't help (sensory data—what I saw and heard). I thought you meant that kindly, yet I thought Sue may have heard it as criticism (my interpretations). I feel concerned (feelings) and would like to clarify with Sue how she heard that (wants). Sue, did you hear Joe's remark as critical of you (your action)?'

"The importance of resolving conflict in groups was mentioned at an earlier meeting. Structuring communications through the Awareness Wheel can be a useful start in resolving conflicts. Asking members in conflict to share awareness and negotiate wants may often result in a satisfactory compromise. Misunderstandings may be cleared up by sharing more complete awareness.

"Stress the use of self-responsible language (the use of 'I' rather than 'you' messages) in presenting the Awareness Wheel. Owning your awareness encourages other members of your group to own theirs. An 'I' message communicates to group members that you respect their integrity by not speaking for them. It demonstrates your trust in the group by showing that you are willing to risk owning and sharing your perceptions."

Exercise: Ask members to divide into groups of two. Ask one member of the group to share his or her awareness of an issue he or she is dealing with, using the Awareness Wheel. Ask the receiving partner to then respond using his or her Awareness Wheel. Discuss what was easy and what was hard. Ask, "Were there parts of your wheel you had difficulty getting in touch with?"

Homework: Practice tuning in to your internal awareness, using the Awareness Wheel structure during the next week.

SESSION 4

- *A. Rounds*

- *B. Questions*

Ask if anyone has questions about the training so far or observations to share. If questions come up during rounds, write them down to address during this part of the session. Before answering questions, ask group members for comments about them. This is an instance when sharing knowledge illustrates the principles of self-help by demonstrating that answers and important contributions can come from members and are not the exclusive domain of one leader.

- *C. Awareness Wheel Review*

Structuring your communication with the Awareness Wheel, describe your perception of the group. Invite members to do the same.

- *D. Feelings: Lecturette*

"Most self-help groups deal with feelings. Basically, feelings are energy. If you view feelings from this frame of reference, dealing with feelings becomes a matter of using energy constructively for problem solving. There are basically four feelings; other 'feeling' words describe combinations and intensities of the four basic feelings. These four are: anger, sadness, fear, and happiness. Anger is energy produced when we don't have what we want or need. The energy experienced from anger can be used to solve problems, to develop options for getting wants or needs met. It is important that people always consider more than one option; good problem solving will generate several options.

"Fear results from a lack of information or a perceived or actual threat to one's well-being. When fear relates to a threat, it is important to determine if the threat is actual or imagined. If actual, the energy is available to take immediate action. If it is imagined, we need to examine the thinking or the basis for that imagining: Are other feelings, perhaps anger, present? When fear is based on a lack of information, the antidote is to seek the necessary information. If this is not entirely possible, using imagination to generate possibilities for handling the feared situation may be helpful. Role playing is a way of stimulating the imagination.

"Sadness is the feeling experienced when we give up on something (real or imagined) that is important to us. It is often experienced as a "slow down". The intensity of the feeling will vary according to the loss. Its range may extend from grief over the death of a loved one to mild sadness at the loss of an opportunity. When experiencing sadness, people need strokes and understanding from others. The needs of survivors deserve special attention at the time of death and are often neglected. Such neglect compounds feelings of sadness. It is important to know the feeling will not last forever. At the resolution of the process, it becomes useful to put energy into looking for ways to fill voids left by the loss and to create positive fantasies of the future.

"Happiness is the energy involved in anticipating or experiencing a pleasurable event. Happiness or joy is the one feeling that may be identified as good. The practice of labeling feelings as good or bad has the effect of encouraging people to deny bad feelings. Feelings are neither good nor bad. Feelings are energy, and the energy needs to be used to gain relief. Relief is the state of equilibrium that one experiences when the energy of the feeling has been dealt with effectively. It is the body's cue that the problem solving was adequate.

"This diagram presents a structure for looking at and dealing with feelings:

"Feeling = Energy -----▶ Problem Solving -----▶ Action = Relief.

"That is, feelings are energy that can be used to solve problems. The problem solving should result in an action which leads to relief. If relief is not achieved, the individual needs to return to the problem-solving point and reevaluate solutions until one is found that leads to relief."

• *E. Interventions: Lecturette and Exercise*

"The facilitator does not have total responsibility for making a self-help group effective. However, early in the group's history, members will look to the facilitator to model ways of dealing with difficult situations. In this training we hope to sharpen facilitator skills in helping the group to meet its goals and deal constructively with problems that may arise. The facilitator needs to be attuned to and thinking about three separate areas of need—the needs of the group, the needs of individual members, and his or her own needs. The process of facilitating in problem solving involves making decisions about which area of need will be addressed and how addressing that area of need will have an impact on the other two areas of need. As far as possible, the facilitator should make her or his thinking about group problems available to the group. The Awareness Wheel is an excellent tool for structuring this process. The facilitator who attempts to solve group problems outside the group is setting himself or herself apart from the group. Such behavior hampers the group's development of interdependency and places the facilitator in an overly responsible position.

"The following questions provide a format that utilizes the Awareness Wheel and takes into account the three areas of need—the group's, the individual member's, and the facilitator's.

1. What do I hear, see, feel, physically?
2. What do I think? (How do I interpret what I hear, see and feel?)
3. What feelings (emotions) do I have?
4. What do I want or wish for myself, for the group, for an individual or individuals in the group?
5. What are all my options?
6. Will the options offer relief to me and to group members?
7. What might the long-term consequences be?
8. What will I do?

"Sharing your answers to questions 1-4 with the group is often a viable option."

EXERCISE

Divide into small groups to work on common problems that arise in groups. In doing this, one further consideration needs to be emphasized. We human beings have a multitude of reasons for behaving as we do. We rarely have just *one* reason for a behavior. In working with people whose behaviors are causing difficulties within a group, it is easy to define the behaviors in judgmental and limiting terms—for example, "Joan talks incessantly in the group because she is inconsiderate of others." In problem solving, it is useful either to suspend judgments or to consider that there are probably many contributing motives for any one behavior.

As a faciliatator you may wish to model caring by assuming that people whose behaviors create problems are caring and capable, and will be invested in changing if they are aware of the impact of their behavior. A problem-solving step may be geared to helping others gain this awareness without communicating judgments which will produce defensiveness.

DIRECTIONS TO GROUP MEMBERS

"On a piece of paper, write a description of a problem situation that you have either encountered in a group or are concerned that you will encounter. Some examples are the person who talks incessantly, the person who never talks, the person who is making angry or deprecating remarks to another member, and the person who consistently arrives late and disrupts the meeting. Pass the descriptions in as you write them. Give only basic details. We can fabricate the missing information as we work on the problems.

"Next, divide into groups of about four members. Each small group will draw four problem situations. The task of each small group will be to discuss these issues one at a time. Following the format in the lecture and using its questions, imagine what your internal awareness would be if you were the facilitator in a group with that problem. As a group, try to devise at least two alternative ways of dealing with each problem. Structure your interventions and role play your first choice with one member acting as facilitator and the others role playing group members reacting to the solution to the problem. What do you think group response might be? Do as many of the four problem situations as you can in the time allowed.

"After each small group has worked on their individual problems, bring the groups together and ask for reports. Discuss reports as time allows."

- *F. Homework*

"Session 5 is a practice session. Each of you—with the exception of the members who facilitated rounds in Session 3—is to find a partner and decide on an activity you want to do with the group. It may be a structured exercise, a discussion, or a form of rounds. During the next session you are to use the group as a setting in which to practice your facilitator skills. (If the group is large, it can be divided into two practice groups running simultaneously.) In planning your exercise, please consider the following:

What type of group would you use this exercise in?

When would you use it?
How much time will you need? (The practice session will have an arbitrary cut-off time. In actual practice the exercise may run longer.)
What will group members gain from the exercise?
What is your task in facilitating this exercise?"

You should tell members that you are willing to meet between training sessions to help them plan their practice exercise.

SESSION 5

- *A. Rounds*

- *B. Facilitating Skills: Practice*

This part of the session is devoted to the practicing of facilitating skills by members of the group. They will have prepared for it according to the homework assignment you gave them at the preceding meeting. (Part F of the guide material for Session 4. Each member team is given a certain amount of time, depending on the number of teams and the length of the session. When planning, allow time for feedback. If necessary, the practice session may extend into Session 6. Each team is given the opportunity to receive feedback from the practice group about the effectiveness of their facilitating. The feedback is to be structured. First, the practice facilitators are asked to comment on how the experience was for them. What was easy; what was hard? Then, the group is asked to give feedback about the skills they saw being used: which were helpful, which might have been done differently?

SESSION 6

- ### A. Continue Practicing Facilitating Skills if Necessary.
- ### B. Problem-Solving Techniques: Lecturette and Exercise

"Basically, there are two types of problems that may arise in self-help groups. They are (1) group problems, for which the entire group needs to agree on a solution; and (2) individual problems, for which the group acts as a resource to the person with the problem."

GROUP PROBLEMS

"Problems that affect the entire group may be solved by brainstorming. The steps are as follows:

"1. *Problem Definition:* What is the problem to be solved? In defining a problem it is important to arrive at a definition in terms that imply a solution. 'We don't have enough money to continue' does not define a problem in a solvable way. 'How can we generate "X" amount of money?' does. A problem definition that is phrased in terms of 'how to' is directed toward a solution. In defining the problem you may also wish to define the impact the problem has on the group.

"2. *Solution Generation:* Each member of the group thinks of as many solutions to the problem as he or she can. During this step do not allow criticism of the solutions. Encourage members to offer any solution that comes to mind without censoring it internally. Sometimes ask each member to generate one absurd solution: Doing so may free energy that is tied up in censoring. Many absurd solutions contain seeds of practical ones.

"3. *Combine Solutions:* Are there any that can be combined? Do so when possible.

"4. *Evaluation:* Review the list of solutions generated. First ask what is good or useful about each solution. Next ask what concerns group members might have about each. At the end of this process, ask if any more solutions have been thought of. If they have, add and evaluate them.

"5. *Rank Ordering:* Ask participants to rank the solutions. For example, have 10 solutions—10 may be for the best and one for the worst.

"6. *Select the Best Solution:* Assign tasks. Who will do what as far as implementation? When will tasks be accomplished? How and when will an evaluation of success take place?"

INDIVIDUAL PROBLEMS

"In regard to solving the problem of an individual, the first step should be to ask the person presenting the problem if she or he wants ideas from the group. It may be that the person simply wants to talk and be heard. In that case, if the group gets into offering solutions, the result will likely be frustration for all involved. If the individual wants ideas from the group, the next step is to ask: How is this a problem? What solutions have you tried? What is your desired outcome? These questions communicate the assumption that the individual presenting the problem is competent, capable, and more knowledgeable about the situation than other people in the group. If these questions are neglected, the group may waste time and energy proposing solutions that have been tried already or ones that do not lead to the desired outcomes."

EXERCISE: BRAINSTORMING

If time permits, the group may practice brainstorming. On the other hand, time may be lacking because you may need to continue the practice of facilitating skills begun in Session 5.

If you have time for brainstorming, solicit a problem from the group that many members share—for example, getting new members. Run through the brainstorming steps. At the completion of the exercise, spend a few minutes to discuss it, using questions such as:

How did the group experience the exercise?
Was the format useful?
What was most useful?
What could have been done differently?

• *C. Evaluation: Discussion*

Since this is the last session, it is useful to evaluate the program in terms of course goals and objectives and individual goals and expectations. The following steps are useful in evaluation:

Review the course goals and objectives.

In rounds, ask members to review their goals and expectations.

Then discuss:

Which of the goals, objectives, expectations were met?

Which were exceeded?

Were there areas of the program that should have been changed?

How should they be changed to improve future training?

• *D. Goodbyes: Lecturette and Exercise*

"Some groups may have a predetermined length, such as this one. Other groups are open-ended. Although members may come and go, the group remains. In any event there is a need to deal with goodbyes or endings. Endings usually contain both sadness and happiness—sadness in the sense of loss of the group or group member and happiness in the anticipation of the future. Members need closure—a sense of letting go—when saying goodbye. One structure for obtaining closure is an exercise in which people exchange regrets and appreciations."

DIRECTIONS FOR EXERCISE

In this exercise regrets are offered first in a round. Clarify with the group that regrets are to be stated with the purpose of letting go. That means that group members do not need to "fix" things for persons having regrets about something in the group's experience; they do not need to judge regrets. Trying to find remedies would be to create a fantasy that the group is not ending or that the group was responsible for being "all things to all people." After regrets, continue with a round of appreciations. After appreciations, ask members to take time to say individual goodbyes.

Appendixes

Appendix 1

TRAINING PROFESSIONALS
IN ORGANIZING SELF-HELP GROUPS*
By Frances J. Dory and Frank Riessman

Most of the general principles for organizing self-help groups will apply to both lay people and professionals. There are, however, some specific issues that professionals need to address. Most critically, the professional role must change as the mutual aid group develops. Initially, the professional can be a generator, a catalyst, or an organizer of the group, and there are multiple models that professionals play in these roles. But as the mutual aid group develops, the professional must shift her or his responsibilities so that the group increasingly develops autonomy, independence, and its own power. Thus the professional must become disengaged from his or her more energetic initial role.

The professional organizer must consider this issue from the beginning, because professionals them-

---

*From *Citizen Participation*, January/February 1982, pp. 27-28. Used by permission.

selves frequently tend to encourage dependent client relationships. This tendency must be broken if the self-help group is to succeed and to become an authentic mutual support unit. Early in the group development process, the professional needs particularly to be alert to seek out energetic people who will energize the group and permit the professional to be a facilitator rather than a leader. The professional must be prepared to become disengaged either completely or gradually from the group, or to move out into other roles as a member of the board, consultant, advisor, sponsor, trainer, sounding board, or occasional visitor.

What are the possible roles of professionals working with self-help groups? One model is to see the professional as a facilitator of new groups. Professionals, however, typically have not been trained for this role—to perceive a need, help establish a self-help group to fill the need, and then to disengage from the group. Special training is required to overcome some of their "trained incapacities."

Another role sees the professional being trained to connect to lay individuals who wish to start a self-help group or need some assistance in relating to groups that already exist. Here there is less danger of the professional usurping control, developing or maintaining dependence, or "professionalizing a non-professional movement." The kind of assistance that would be provided would range from group development and process skills to public relations skills. The professional might help the group acquire needed resources and improve linkages to the formal caregiving system. On the spot, direct consultation to the group might be provided occasionally.

The following are some suggestions for training professionals to work with self-help groups:

• Have professionals attend open meetings of existing self-help groups, particularly AA and Recovery, Inc., and also chapters of groups that they might be helping to form.

• Simulate self-help groups in the training process.

• Have some sessions in the training process include members of self-help groups, films of self-help groups, or presentations by members of self-help groups.

• Have discussions of the "self-help way" in contrast to the professional way, and directed toward raising consciousness and away from the need to control the group.

• Present case histories of professionals working with self-help groups, with particular emphasis on various critical decision points, e.g., entry, developing a contract, disengaging, dealing with a group that is "stuck."

• Help the professional to accept that there is a natural, useful tension between self-help groups and the professional.

• Help the professional to learn how to spot leadership and to encourage it.

• Conduct most of the training in an experimental fashion with minimal didactic presentation.

• Help the professional to assess the organizational setting in which he or she works and the issues involved in introducing self-help groups in the particular setting—how to overcome resistance and develop strategy.

• Encourage the professional to join a self-help group and to reflect on this participation, as well as to reflect on participation in previous self-help groups of which she or he was a member.

• Review the many ways in which professionals have related to self-help groups and provide various examples (Recovery, Inc., Parents Anonymous, peer counseling groups, Florida Mental Health Institute, SHARE, widow groups, Families of the Mentally Ill, Community Service Society, American Cancer Society, MASH, Compassionate Friends, Mended Hearts, the Fortune Society).

There are other factors to be considered when organizing a self-help or mutual aid group. Some of these are examined below.

In developing a mutual aid group it may be useful in the first phase to seek out a task force of potentially interested people to consider what the group will be like—goals, norms, practices, methodology, rationale, need for the group, potential clientele, ways of reaching other people, needed resources, logistics, etc. Remember that in the first stages of group formation things do not move rapidly, and if one expects quick results one is likely to become disappointed and frustrated. One of the most important things that happens in the first phase is that the people get to know each other, enjoy each other, and start to build the group process. It's important not to go too fast but to build traditions slowly and carefully.

Consider carefully what the payoffs may be for the members in the group and try to build them in where possible. Payoffs include enjoying the group process, getting to know people, becoming removed from isolation and alienation, developing networks, having a connection to the agency and the professional, doing something, filling time, helping other people, acquiring skills, getting a feeling of importance and identity, learning how to deal with problems and needs, developing coping strategies, getting feedback and a "mirror," acquiring friends, acquiring feeling of empowerment or control over one's own life, getting the benefits of support, rapping, and catharsis.

It is probably true that if a self-help group does not grow, it will die or wither away. This point is related to the well-known self-help idea that in order to have something you have to give it away. In other words, you have to help other people in order to be helped yourself. You have to model and reaffirm. But it's also important to recall that there is considerable turnover in many self-help groups and that people come and go, very often in a rather loose fashion.

Mutual aid groups usually have a mission, an ideology or persuasion strategy, a rationale and a methodology or practice. These dimensions, of course, do not develop overnight, but it may be useful to keep an eye out for them and perhaps to raise questions around these dimensions as the groups develop.

Self-help groups vary enormously in their style or manner of functioning. Some require anonymity, some do not. Some have an advocacy orientation, while others insist that the problems are internal to the members and do not require any social or legislative intervention. Some are proprietary, some are not. Some have very specific methodologies like AA's Twelve Steps and its Twelve Rules, while others are much looser. Some are eager to expand, others are not. Some accept government support while others prefer to raise money in different ways. Some are pro-professional, others anti-professional or adversarial. Thus, it is important to get some understanding of what style might appeal to the potential membership that is to be recruited. Obviously, this cannot be anticipated in advance. The organizer must be receptive to cues, and it would be useful to have knowledge of a wide variety of self-help repertoires and stylings to see which might best fit the group that is emerging.

Leadership in most self-help groups is shared, often rotating, and the structures typically are not hierarchical. The professional should have an eye out for the different kinds of leadership roles that may emerge: energizer, old-timer, group-cohesion builder, chairperson, fund raiser, trainer, model, representative to the outside world, mobilizer, interpreter, recruiter, helper, innovator, or manager.

The professional, in his or her roles in the group as consultant, advisor, etc. should be concerned that the group may be getting stale, members getting burned out, with a general drift downward, suggesting a need for revitalization, and self-evaluation.

With these suggestions in mind, professionals working with self-help groups can maximize their contributions.

Appendix 2

The two optional worksheets that follow are the product of advanced facilitator seminars. As people begin facilitating groups, new issues often arise along with old issues in new forms. Since few self-help group facilitators have extensive backgrounds in group work, some structured ongoing training is very useful. *Leading Self-Help Groups* covers only the basic training. Ongoing support groups for facilitators—where members share concerns, solutions, and learnings—are highly recommended.

FACILITATOR AWARENESS
A Worksheet

1) A good group facilitator always . . .
    (list 3)
    A.
    B.
    C.
2) A good facilitator should never . . .
    (list 2)
    A.
    B.

3) _____ would never happen if a facilitator were on the ball.
4) My greatest fear in being a facilitator is _____.
5) My greatest hope about being a facilitator is _____.

6) List five traits of a good facilitator:
   A.
   B.
   C.
   D.
   E.

BURNOUT
A Worksheet

Burnout is the condition in which the stresses and negatives in a situation outweigh positives and continue to do so for a prolonged length of time without relief or the hope for relief.

Who "burns out"? Caring people who have entered a situation with hope and positive intentions.

Symptoms of burnout:

Lack of energy and enthusiasm
Low level anger
Frustration
Sense of futility
Lack of goals

Causes of burnout in group leaders:

Lack of clear role definition
Lack of achievable role definition

Lack of strokes
Isolation
Failure to set limits
Lack of recognition of one's labor

Solution to burnout:

Working in teams or small committees
Periodic time off
Delegation of responsibilities
Frequent contact with other group leaders to discuss issues
Setting up a system for strokes
Clear-cut job description that is:
- specific
- reasonable
- achievable
- time limited

A working understanding of concept of "rescuing"
Recognition of one's own limits
Meeting one's own survival needs
Relations in which one gets as well as gives
Having a safe place to ventilate or share feelings

Questions:

What can you do now to avoid that?
If you are presently experiencing burnout, what are some action steps you can take?